TERRY STREET

DOUGLAS DUNN

Terry Street

faber and faber
LONDON · BOSTON

First published in 1969
by Faber and Faber Limited
3 Queen Square London WC1N 3AU
First published in this paperback edition 1971
Reissued in 1986

Printed in Great Britain by
Redwood Burn Ltd
Trowbridge Wiltshire

ISBN 0 571 09176 8 (hardback)
ISBN 0 571 09713 8 (paperback)

For

LESLEY

ACKNOWLEDGEMENTS

Some of these poems have appeared in the following magazines or anthologies: *Times Literary Supplement; The London Magazine; The New Statesman; The Listener; The Review; Stand; Universities Poetry; Scottish Poetry 4* (Edinburgh U.P.); *Poetry Introduction* (Faber). 'Close of Play' was read on the BBC's 'Poetry Now'.

CONTENTS

PART ONE: Terry Street Poems

PART TWO

9

PART I

TERRY STREET POEMS

THE CLOTHES PIT

The young women are obsessed with beauty.
Their old fashioned sewing machines rattle in Terry
    Street.
They must keep up, they must keep up.

They wear teasing skirts and latest shoes,
Lush, impermanent coats, American cosmetics.
But they lack intellectual grooming.

In the culture of clothes and little philosophies,
They only have clothes. They do not need to be seen
Carrying a copy of *International Times,*

Or the Liverpool Poets, the wish to justify their looks
With things beyond themselves. They mix up colours,
And somehow they are often fat and unlovely.

They don't get high on pot, but get sick on cheap
Spanish Burgundy, or beer in rampant pubs,
And come home supported and kissed and bad-tempered.

But they have clothes, bright enough to show they dream
Of places other than this, an inarticulate paradise,
Eating exotic fowl in sunshine with courteous boys.

Three girls go down the street with the summer wind.
The litter of pop rhetoric blows down Terry Street,
Bounces past their feet, into their lives.

NEW LIGHT ON TERRY STREET

First sunshine for three weeks, and children come out
From their tents of chairs and old sheets,

Living room traffic jams, and battlefields of redcoat soldiers,
To expand, run with unsteady legs in and out of shades.

Up terraces of slums, young gum-chewing mothers sit
Outside on their thrones of light. Their radios,

Inside or placed on window ledges, grow hot
With sun and electricity. Shielding their eyes from sun

They talk above music, knitting or pushing prams
Over gentle, stone inches. Under clawed chairs

Cats sleep in the furry shade. Children bounce balls
Up into their dreams of sand, and the sea they have not seen.

Becoming tired, the fascination of wheels takes them.
They pedal their trikes slowly through dust in hollows,

Quietly give up cheek to old men, sing with sly voices.
A half-heard love song idles on the wind.

Suddenly it is empty as life without the great ambitions.
Like living in a deep, dried-up riverbed, a throat that
      thirsts.

Yet there is no unrest. The dust is so fine.
You hardly notice you have grown too old to cry out for
      change.

THE PATRICIANS

In small backyards old men's long underwear
Drips from sagging clotheslines.
The other stuff they take in bundles to the Bendix.

There chatty women slot their coins and joke
About the grey unmentionables absent.
The old men weaken in the steam and scratch at their rough
    chins.

Suppressing coughs and stiffnesses, they pedal bikes
On low gear slowly, in their faces
The effort to be upright, a dignity

That fits inside the smell of aromatic pipes.
Walking their dogs, the padded beats of pocket watches,
Muffled under ancient overcoats, silences their hearts.

They live watching each other die, passing each other
In their white scarves, too long known to talk,
Waiting for the inheritance of the oldest, a right to power.

The street's patricians, they are ignored.
Their anger proves something, their disenchantments
Settle round me like a cold fog.

They are the individualists of our time.
They know no fashions, copy nothing but their minds.
Long ago, they gave up looking in mirrors.

Dying in their sleep, they lie undiscovered.
The howling of their dogs brings the sniffing police,
Their middle-aged children from the new estates.

MEN OF TERRY STREET

They come in at night, leave in the early morning.
I hear their footsteps, the ticking of bicycle chains,
Sudden blasts of motorcycles, whimpering of vans.
Somehow I am either in bed, or the curtains are drawn.

This masculine invisibility makes gods of them,
A pantheon of boots and overalls.
But when you see them, home early from work
Or at their Sunday leisure, they are too tired

And bored to look long at comfortably.
It hurts to see their faces, too sad or too jovial.
They quicken their step at the smell of cooking,
They hold up their children and sing to them.

INCIDENT IN THE SHOP

Not tall, her good looks unstylised,
She wears no stockings, or uses cosmetic.

I sense beneath her blouse
The slow expanse of unheld breasts.

I feel the draughts on her legs,
The nip of cheap detergent on her hands.

Under her bed, forgotten winter bulbs
Die of thirst, in the grip of a wild dust.

Her husband beats her. Old women
Talk of it behind her back, watching her.

She buys the darkest rose I ever saw
And tucks its stem into her plastic belt.

THE TERRY STREET FUSILIERS

Wide-bottomed trousers flap in the east wind.
In a long, belted raincoat, his hair cut short,
He limps with a stick faster than I walk.
If Terry Street was attacked, he would defend us
With the bread knife, jumping out from doorways.
This quiet man, this veteran of wars,
Goes boyish off to shop in the cheapest streets,
Proud and upright, setting his example.
I must walk straighter, lose a little weight.

A REMOVAL FROM TERRY STREET

On a squeaking cart, they push the usual stuff,
A mattress, bed ends, cups, carpets, chairs,
Four paperback westerns. Two whistling youths
In surplus U.S. Army battle-jackets
Remove their sister's goods. Her husband
Follows, carrying on his shoulders the son
Whose mischief we are glad to see removed,
And pushing, of all things, a lawnmower.
There is no grass in Terry Street. The worms
Come up cracks in concrete yards in moonlight.
That man, I wish him well. I wish him grass.

ON ROOFS OF TERRY STREET

Television aerials, Chinese characters
In the lower sky, wave gently in the smoke.

Nest-building sparrows peck at moss,
Urban flora and fauna, soft, unscrupulous.

Rain drying on the slates shines sometimes.
A builder is repairing someone's leaking roof.

He kneels upright to rest his back.
His trowel catches the light and becomes precious.

FROM THE NIGHT-WINDOW

The night rattles with nightmares.
Children cry in the close-packed houses,
A man rots in his snoring.
On quiet feet, policemen test doors.
Footsteps become people under streetlamps.
Drunks return from parties,
Sounding of empty bottles and old songs.
Young women come home,
And disappear into white beds
At the edge of the night.
All windows open, this hot night,
And the sleepless, smoking in the dark,
Making small red lights at their mouths,
Count the years of their marriages.

SUNDAY MORNING AMONG THE HOUSES OF TERRY STREET

On the quiet street, Saturday night's fag-packets,
Balls of fish and chip newspaper, bottles
Placed neatly on window sills, beside cats.

A street of oilstains and parked motorbikes,
Wet confectionery wrappers becoming paste,
Things doing nothing, ending, rejected.

Revellers return tieless, or with hairdos deceased,
From parties, paying taxis in the cold,
Unsmiling in the fogs of deflated mirth.

Neighbours in pyjamas watch them from upstairs,
Chewing on pre-breakfast snacks,
Waiting for kettles to boil, wives quit the lav.

Men leave their beds to wash and eat,
Fumble with Sunday papers and radio knobs,
Leaving in their beds their wives and fantasies,

In bedside cups their teeth, their smiles.
Drinkers sleep into a blank sobriety,
Still talking to the faces in the smoke,

Women they regretted they were too drunk to touch,
Sucking tastes in their mouths, their mossy teeth.
Into the street come early-risen voices,

The Salvation Army's brass dulled in sunlessness
And breath of singers the colour of tubas.
Dog obbligatos rise from warm corners.

Behind the houses, antique plumbing
Coughs and swallows Sunday morning's flush
Down to Hull's underworld, its muddy roots.

A city of disuse, a sink, a place,
Without people it would be like the sea-bottom.
Beneath the street, a thundering of mud.

LATE NIGHT WALK DOWN TERRY STREET

A policeman on a low-powered motorcycle stops.
His radio crackles, his helmet yellows.

Empty buses heading for the depot
Rush past the open end of Terry Street.

In their light, a man with a bike walking home,
Too drunk to ride it, turns into Terry Street.

Taxis swerve down Terry Street's shortcut,
Down uneven halls of Street Lighting Department yellow.

Into which now comes the man with the bike,
Struggling to keep on his legs.

The policeman waits under a gone-out streetlamp.
He stops the drunk, they talk, they laugh together.

I pass them then, beside dark, quiet houses,
In others mumbling sounds of entertainment;

Cathode-glows through curtains, faint latest tunes;
Creaking of bedsprings, lights going out.

AFTER CLOSING TIME

Here they come, the agents of rot,
The street tarts and their celebrating trawlermen,
Singing or smoking, carrying bottles,
In a staggered group ten minutes before snow.

WINTER

Recalcitrant motorbikes;
Dog-shit under frost; a coughing woman;
The old men who cannot walk briskly groaning
On the way back from their watchmen's huts.

INS AND OUTS

The dustmen spread the worst rumours.
Postmen tell their friends how little mail
We get, only buff envelopes with windows,
Football pools, advertising for baby foods,
Ribald postcards from Brid and Blackpool.

But the dustmen tell other stories.
Pretending where they live is not as bad as this,
They say to their wives how our garbage
Is all potato peelings and crisp-packets,
Bean tins, cheap wine empties and chip shop newspapers.

In the sunless dustbin alleys, vermin devour cats;
Old women are seen wiping in doorless toilets;
Layers of smell flake off the air like invisible soot;
French letters cool, relics of life-hot winter shags;
And a girlie mag breaks up in glossy fragments,
Focus of masturbation by torchlight, among hungry cats.

The postmen see the fronts of us, poverty and bills,
The proofs we are administered.
The dustmen, red-eyed with lifting, and ash-coloured,
See the back sides of us, the bits we don't paint,
And keep children out of with warnings of dogs and fever.

First thing on Mondays, their scuffling boots
Unease us, removing the debris of our cooking
And possessions, getting to know us from the leanness
Of our rubbish, and the litter left by furtive night-visitors,
Mistakenly thinking that we're different.

YOUNG WOMEN IN ROLLERS

Because it's wet, the afternoon is quiet.
Children, pacified with sweets inside
Their small houses, stroke travelling cats
From the kingdom of dustbins and warm smells.

Young women come to visit their married friend.
Waiting for their hair to set beneath thin scarves,
They walk about in last year's fashions,
Stockingless, in coats and old shoes.

They look strong, white-legged creatures
With nothing to do but talk of what it is to love
And sing words softly to the new tunes,
The type who burst each other's blackheads

In the street and look in handbag mirrors
While they walk, not talking of the weather,
Who call across the street they're not wearing knickers,
But blush when they pass you alone.

This time they see me at my window, among books,
A specimen under glass, being protected,
And laugh at me watching them.
They minuet to Mozart playing loudly

On the afternoon Third. They mock me thus,
They mime my softness. A landlord stares.
All he has worked for is being destroyed.
The slum rent-masters are at one with Pop.

The movements they imagine go with minuet
Stay patterned on the air. I can see soot,
It floats. The whiteness of their legs has changed
Into something that floats, become like cloth.

They disappear into the house they came to visit.
Out of the open door rush last year's hits,
The music they listen to, that takes up their time
In houses that are monuments to entertainment.

I want to be touched by them, know their lives,
Dance in my own style, learn something new.
At night, I even dream of ideal communities.
Why do they live where they live, the rich and the poor?

Tonight, when their hair is ready, after tea,
They'll slip through laws and the legs of policemen.
I won't be there, I'll be reading books elsewhere.
There are many worlds, there are many laws.

A DEATH IN TERRY STREET

There are some old women who want to live here
   forever,
But if they are to die, this is the place for it.
They take a pride in dying where they always lived,
Preferably tended by sons, and neighbours with soup.

If Terry Street was the only place,
They could not be disposed of here,
Unless men dug through brick and concrete,
Or lowered them into drains, burned them in their yards,
Raised them on tall scaffolds for the birds to eat,
Or cut them up and flushed them down the toilets.
Eventually, they might find words to say
That fitted these new ceremonies, the old men
Having stayed in for days, leafing through dictionaries.
What a thing that would be, the complete place,
With priests and undertakers, livestock and fields.

From the shapeless street, a bad address,
The black cars take her to a better district.
The neighbours watch her go, from doorways and windows,
Learning a lesson of all times and men,
That when you die you have to leave,
And walk with giant footsteps from the street
That is like dark cliffs of sand,
Mocking the sanitary inspectors, bypassing the housing list.

THE SILENCES

It is urban silence, it is not true silence.
The main road, growling in the distance,
Continuous, is absorbed into it;
The birds, their noises become lost in it;
Faint, civilised music decorates it.

These are edges round a quiet centre where lives are lived,
Children brought up, where television aerial fixers come,
Or priests on black bikes to lecture the tardy.
If you turn your back on it, people are only noises,
Coughs, footsteps, conversations, hands working.

They are a part of the silence of places,
The people who live here, working, falling asleep,
In a place removed one style in time outwith
The trend of places. They are like a lost tribe.
The dogs bark when strangers come, with rent books, or
    free gifts.

They move only a little from where they are fixed.
Looking at worn clothes, they sense impermanence.
They have nothing to do with where they live, the silence
    tells them.
They have looked at it so long, with such disregard,
It is baked now over their eyes like a crust.

A WINDOW AFFAIR

We were looking at the same things,
Men on bikes, the litter round the drain,
The sparrows eating in the frozen shade.

We heard the same inweave of random noise,
The chant of children's games, and waiting cars
Of salesmen and collectors ticking over.

This was weekday flirtation, through the glass,
The love of eyes and silence, in which you cannot touch
Or talk, a useless love for the bored and tired.

Her window caught the winter sun and shone.
I imagined everything, the undressing, love,
The coy sleep. But there was nothing to say.

There were two faces, and they passed each other
Like shillings in circulation. Untouchable,
She was far away, in a world of foul language,

Two children, the television set in the corner,
As common as floral wallpaper or tea,
Her husband in at six to feed the greyhounds.

I used to crave the ideal life of Saturdays and Sundays,
A life of everything in a gay, short-lived country
Of high-living among the northern bricks,

Where people come out rested into the rain,
Wearing smiles as if they were expensive clothes,
Their bodies clean and warm and their jobs indoors.

But some ideals have passed far out of my reach,
The goodwill became full of holes like a sieve.
I grasp only the hard things, windows, contempt.

I could not kiss that face, the glowing mask
Of those who have been too much entertained,
That laughs the sour laugh and smells of food.

It's come to this, that in this time, this place,
There is a house I feel I have to leave,
Because my life is cracked, and in a room

Stares out of windows at a window face,
Thin shifts of dust on the sunning glass,
And does not want to love, and does not care.

PART II

THE WORST OF ALL LOVES

Where do they go, the faces, the people seen
In glances and longed for, who smile back
Wondering where the next kiss is coming from?

They are seen suddenly, from the top decks of buses,
On railway platforms at the tea machine,
When the sleep of travelling makes us look for them.

A whiff of perfume, an eye, a hat, a shoe,
Bring back vague memories of names,
Thingummy, that bloke, what's-her-name.

What great thing have I lost, that faces in a crowd
Should make me look at them for one I know,
What are faces that they must be looked for?

But there's one face, seen only once,
A fragment of a crowd. I know enough of her.
That face makes me dissatisfied with myself.

Those we secretly love, who never know of us,
What happens to them? Only this is known.
They will never meet us suddenly in pleasant rooms.

TRIBUTE OF A LEGS LOVER

They are my dancing girls, the wasted lives,
The chorus girls who do not make good,
Who are not given florist's shops or Schools of Dance
By rich and randy admirers, or marry
A gullible Joe from Swindon or Goole,
But find themselves stiff and rotten at fifty,
With bad legs, and no money to pay for the taxi,
Outside cheap drinking places on Grand National day.

THE SEASON FOR HATS

The streamlined women are coming into heat.
From winters cooked up with their husbands
They come out to walk alone in the park,
With the poodle perhaps, or the book in fashion.

And they smile at the young men, and may even talk
For five minutes, about the book they're reading.
Then they suddenly remember something, and run off.
The young man cannot forget her hat, or her fear.

BRING OUT YOUR DEAD

A cart goes by, the creaking wheels of peace,
Loaded up with old cookers and discarded clothes.
The widows finally threw out their husbands' suits,
On their way to decadence, remarriage, or classic grief.

The driver sings, a child teases him with an old boot.
Man and boy, they take away the used, discarded heap.
A widow looks in the empty wardrobe, at mothballs
Like old fondant sweets, a pair of shoes she missed.

CLOSE OF PLAY

Cricketers have the manners of ghosts,
Wandering in white on the tended ground.

They go in now, walking in twos and threes.
This sight is worth a week of evenings.

Players' wives and girlfriends put away tea-flasks,
Start complaining of goosepimples.

Nearby, the vicious pluck of unseen tennis,
A harrier contesting the park its contours,

Fighting a hill with rhythmic blue shoes.
Behind the trees, toughminded fops

In sports cars roar like a mini-Bacchus,
Their girls toss back their summer hair.

The sweet-smelling suburbs cool, settle.
Their people hesitate in the gap before night.

Now it is getting dark, they go indoors.
They do not dance by firelight on their lawns.

Inside, daughters practice one last scale,
Sober sons of teachers learn another fact.

Armchairs surround the tired, the lustful
Absorb their beds. On the garden table,

In the unrotting glasses, dregs of whisky
Or martini become alive, golden smells.

Gardens aspire to wildness in the dark,
The cricket fields grow defiantly, reach up,

Trees become less polite. The groundsman's roller
Tries to crash screaming into the pavilion.

Out of the webs of ivy, silent as smoke,
Comes the wildness of the always growing,

The menace of unplanned shoots, the brick-eaters.
From taps and cisterns, water, the wild country,

Flows through bungalows and villas.
Damp corners grow moss. The golf course

Becomes a desert, a place without mannners.
The rapists gather under hedges and bridges.

HORSES IN A SUBURBAN FIELD

The road-dust settles behind the hedges
That enclose the small suburban fields.
Trees stand in straight lines, planted
By noblemen with an eye for order,
Trees in a park sold off to pay death duty.
Discarded things rot on the ground,
Paper shifts in the wind, metals rust.
Children play in the grass, like snakes,
Out of the way, on headache-soothing absences.

Sad and captured in a towny field,
The horses peep through the light,
Step over the tin cans, a bicycle frame.
They stand under a dried-up hawthorn
With dust on its leaves, smell distant kitchens.
Then they wander through the dust,
The dead dreams of housewives.

THE LOVE DAY

April, and young women glorify their flesh.
Their blushes warm their lovers' eyes.

The frisky toughs discard their heavy jackets,
Put on dark, sparse muscle-shirts.

Youth walks in couples nervous to cool bedrooms.
Some learn that love is not bad or permanent.

The ruffians are soft with their girlfriends.
They smile, keep their voices down, park their motorbikes.

Spring, the fugitives come to a stop here,
The thrush muffles its voice under the blossom,

Young husbands notice the flower shops,
The old men kiss their wives and long for their children.

It only lasts a day. After it, the insects come out.
Tender hands and mouths go back to eating.

THE SELF-MADE MAN

Take this coat now, that I hold out to you,
In my fingers that are like the stale stubs of cigars.
And fingers, too, that like the feel of fur,
That live in pockets and in bags of sweets;
Indulgent fingers, on hands that have been places,
Murderous in mountain streams, in the gills of fish,
Boyish hands that thieved the mellow orchards.
But now they swim through fur, soft as adultery,
Or reach into wallets for my easy money.

BELLE AND BEAU

I used to watch you coming, from a distance.
This made me remember when I first knew you.
When I saw you coming from a distance,
You were less known to me again. Walking,
Knowing you by your clothes, your style,
All I had ever thought of you came back
With your coming closer. How I had been fooled!
All that time I had been in love with a coat.

INSOMNIA ON ROETZEL'S ISLAND

I long for her, her whimsical face.
The bed breathes its choir of springs as I move.
I see her face like a face beneath the water,
Such is the moonlight of Canada.
The kisses are useless as insect bites.
I forget night with one brushing of teeth.

LOVE POEM

I live in you, you live in me;
We are two gardens haunted by each other.
Sometimes I cannot find you there,
There is only the swing creaking, that you have just left,
Or your favourite book beside the sundial.

END OF THE OLDEST REVOLUTION

Sons sit back, alone in their rooms, after
The social evenings rich with company,
And see in the smoke the faces of the fathers
They look like, whom they lavishly criticized
When they lived at home. Now, at twenty-six,
Only very slightly drunk, they cough
Into their hands, in the cigarette smoke
That trails the lines of faces inside their throats.

NARCISSUS

Vanity, I could dance all night
Down the hall of mirrors with you,
Looking down the cleft in your dress,
(For you must be a woman),

Dipping here and bowing there
To the portraits of my ancestors
That all look remarkably like me,
Their eyes rounded by looking at water.

I would wear glass shoes if I could get them,
To see my face breaking over them,
Thinly reflected above my white feet moving,
My face moving and vanishing as I walk.

I've looked so much in mirrors I could step
Into the soothing presence of myself,
Spectating my own beauty,
Hardly believing I am mine.

If there was an end put to all reflection,
At night you would find me walking
With a burning torch, everywhere,
Looking for whatever I used to find in my face.

A DREAM OF JUDGEMENT

Posterity, thy name is Samuel Johnson.
You sit on a velvet cushion on a varnished throne
Shaking your head sideways, saying No,
Definitely no, to all the books held up to you.
Licking your boots is a small Scotsman
Who looks like Boswell, but is really me.
You go on saying No, quite definitely no,
Adjusting the small volume of Horace
Under your wig and spitting in anger
At the portrait of Blake Swift is holding up.
Quite gently, Pope ushers me out into the hell
Of forgotten books. Nearby, teasingly,
In the dustless heaven of the classics,
There is singing of morals in Latin and Greek.

A DREAM OF RANDOM LOVE

Fond women, walking at the edge of woods,
Waiting for chance lovers, they will not come.

Dressed in long raincoats, with deep pockets,
They turn up their collars at the first rain,

And with long, slow steps walk under a tree.
The grass seed sticks to their wet shoes.

In these woods, I am hunting on a grey horse,
Crossing and recrossing streams after deer.

The one I follow leads me to the forest's end,
Where the daylight presses down the fields

With grey and silver. The mare's breath
Blows back in my face. And women are here,

Some sheltering, and some walking away
Into the high grass, up to their waists in seed,

Wading towards the city, where lines of smoke
Mean there are rooms, and men with empty beds.

Of all these women of an equal, silent beauty,
Does it matter which one I will choose or take?

The one I stop at struggles with her coyness.
Her green eyes shine like water on leaves,

My big, uninterested mare champs grass.
I bend from the saddle and lift her up.

Trees and bushes whip past in the easy gallop,
Water springs off leaves, she presses her cheek on my
    back.

And as the pounding of the hooves fades out,
Riding through the wood, to my cave under the
    waterfall,

I hear myself depart, as though there were two of me.
One is the darkness under trees, one is the light above
    open fields.

THE OCEAN'S LOVE TO RALEGH

I stare with Ralegh's boyhood out to sea,
Looking for an ivory tower that has nothing to do
With God or politics, but everything to do with water.
I think I will mayflower a new land,
Taking old elements to make a new order,

Earth, air, fire, and water, the giddy limits,
The shedding of nationality and death of flags.
And up the Orinoco in my Prospero's cell
Become virtuous, and teach the wildlife tricks,
Writing out my *History of the World,*

Until you, Ralegh, come, with gleaming ships,
A bloodstain on your ruff, and no head.

LANDSCAPE WITH ONE FIGURE

Shipyard cranes have come down again
To drink at the river, turning their long necks
And saying to their reflections on the Clyde,
"How noble we are."

The fields are waiting for them to come over.
Trees gesticulate into the rain,
The nerves of grasses quiver at their tips.
Come over and join us in the wet grass!

The wings of gulls in the distance wave
Like handkerchiefs after departing emigrants.
A tug sniffs up the river, looking like itself.
Waves fall from their small heights on river mud.

If I could sleep standing, I would wait here
For ever, become a landmark, something fixed
For tug crews or seabound passengers to point at,
An example of being a part of a place.

SOUTH BANK OF THE HUMBER

Brickworks, generators of cities, break up
And then descend, sustaining no wages.

A sheet of corrugated iron smacks against a wall,
The wing of a pre-biological, inorganic bird.

It is the laughter of permanence,
The laughter of metal in a brickfield becoming dust.

PASSING THROUGH

We had to start from where our parents put us
Until we met in the lists of coming and going.

Where do they begin, attractions, pity,
And when they're finished, where do they go?

Like water that cupped hands cannot hold,
We passed through each other, we changed, sometimes

We even disappeared, flowing off elsewhere,
Sucked into porous distances, making gaps

That were wider than geography,
Dried up in the sun of consuming loves.

Walking together through spaces other people have filled,
Our edges become hot in the air remembering them.

THE QUEEN OF THE BELGIANS

Commemorating Astrid's death
The Belgians made a postage stamp
That my father prized, for her face.
Like my mother's, Thirties-beautiful,
Serene around its edges.

I've got it in my album now,
A thing handed down, like advice,
For me to find in the face
Of a queen at Europe's edge
What it was my father found.

Queen Astrid, that my father
Put in an album for her face,
Is puffed into my thoughts by love.
It beats there like the heart of all I know.
I am the age my father was.

SHIPS

When a ship passes at night on the Clyde,
Swans in the reeds, picking oil from their feathers,
Look up at the lights, the noise of new waves,
Against hill-climbing houses, malefic cranes.

A fine rain attaches itself to the ship like skin.
Lascars play poker, the Scottish mate looks
At the last lights, one that is Ayrshire,
Others on lonely rocks, or clubfooted peninsulas.

They leave restless boys without work in the river towns.
In their houses are fading pictures of fathers ringed
Among ships' complements in wartime, model destroyers,
Souvenirs from uncles deep in distant engine rooms.

Then the boys go out, down streets that look on water.
They say, "I could have gone with them,"
A thousand times to themselves in the glass cafés,
Over their American soft drinks, into their empty hands.

A POEM IN PRAISE OF THE BRITISH

Regiments of dumb gunners go to bed early.
Soldiers, sleepy after running up and down
Hideaway British Army meadows,
Clean the daisies off their mammoth boots.
The general goes pink in his bath reading
Lives of the Great Croquet Players.
At Aldershot, beside foot-stamping squares,
Young officers drink tea and touch their toes.

Heavy rain everywhere washes up the bones of British.
Where did all that power come from, the wish
To be inert, but rich and strong, to have too much?
Where does glory come from, and when it's gone
Why are old soldiers sour and the bank's empty?
But how sweet is the weakness after Empire
In the garden of a flat, safe country shire,
Watching the beauty of the random, spare, superfluous,

Drifting as if in sleep to the ranks of memorialists
That wait like cabs to take us off down easy street,
To the redcoat armies, and the flags and treaties
In marvellous archives, preserved like leaves in books.
The archivist wears a sword and clipped moustache.
He files our memories, more precious than light,
To be of easy access to politicians of the Right,
Who now are sleeping, like undertakers on black cushions,

Thinking of inflammatory speeches and the adoring mob.
What a time this would be for true decadence!
Walking, new-suited, with trim whiskers, swinging
Our gold-knobbed walking sticks, to the best restaurants;
Or riding in closed black carriages to discreet salons,
To meet the women made by art, the fashionably beautiful;
Or in the garden, read our sonnets by the pool,
Beside small roses, next week's buttonholes.

In this old country, we are falling asleep, under clouds
That are like wide-brimmed hats. This is just right.
Old pederasts on the Brighton promenade
Fall asleep to dream of summer seductions.
The wind blows their hats away, and they vanish
Into archives of light, where greatness has gone,
With the dainty tea cup and the black gun,
And dancing dragoons in the fields of heaven.

COSMOLOGIST

There is something joyful
In the stones today,
An inorganic ringing
At the roots of people.

The back of my hand
With its network of small veins
Has changed to the underside of a leaf.
If water fell on me now
I think I would grow.